Teaching Early Concepts with Photos of Kids

by Beth Geyer and Frank Geyer

NEW YORK • TORONTO • LONDON • AUCKLAND • SYDNEY
MEXICO CITY • NEW DELHI • HONG KONG • BUENOS AIRES

Teaching *Resources*

Acknowledgments

This book would not have been possible without all the wonderful children and families at the Child Development Laboratory at the University of Missouri-Columbia. Special thanks goes to all the children in our Green Door classroom.

◇ ◇ ✶ ◇ ◇ ✦ ◇ ◇ ✶ ◇ ◇ ✦ ◇ ◇ ✶ ◇ ◇

Cover design by Jim Sarfati

Cover photographs by Beth Geyer and Frank Geyer
except for upper left photo © Stockbyte Royalty Free Photos © 1997–2002 Stockbyte™
All rights reserved.

Interior design by Sydney Wright

Interior photographs by Beth Geyer and Frank Geyer

ISBN: 0-439-51770-2
Copyright © 2005 by Beth Geyer and Frank Geyer
Published by Scholastic Inc.
All rights reserved.
Printed in the U.S.A.

4 5 6 7 8 9 10   40   13 12 11 10 09

Contents

Introduction

The early years are an important time in the development of children's perceptions of who they are and how they feel about themselves. Using photographs in the classroom provides a wonderful way to help nurture children's self-esteem, build classroom community, and make learning fun! In this book, you'll find dozens of activities that show how to incorporate children's photographs into your teaching. These unique and creative ideas go beyond decorating the classroom, truly integrating photographs into all areas of the curriculum.

The activities in this book provide hands-on experience, allowing children to learn early concepts and develop key skills through actively exploring and manipulating photographs of themselves and their classmates. The activities give children practice with shapes, numbers, letters, colors, patterns, opposites, graphing, art, movement, and more. Each activity notes the developmental focus it reinforces—cognitive, social/emotional, physical, or creative—and includes simple, step-by-step directions as well as variations and extensions.

Using photographs in our own classroom has been an ongoing process of discovery and learning both for us and for the children we teach. We hope this book will inspire you to begin this discovery process in your classroom as well.

—*Beth Geyer and Frank Geyer*

How to Use This Book

The activities in this book are organized by general topics: early concepts; self-awareness; movement and music; puzzles, puppets, and more. Use the activities in any order and adapt them as you see fit to meet the needs of your students and curriculum. For each activity, you'll find the following sections:

Materials: This lists the materials needed, including any photographs. Please note that the same photographs can be used for many different activities. For this reason, we suggest laminating photographs whenever possible. Activities can also be modified to accommodate available supplies.

Developmental Focus: Each activity notes the main developmental focuses that it reinforces—cognitive, social/emotional, physical, or creative. This section also notes which activities address antibias awareness.

Preparation: Many of the activities require only simple advance preparation, such as cutting photographs to size.

Play: This section provides step-by-step instructions for leading the activity.

Variations and Extensions: Here you'll find suggestions to make activities more or less challenging, or to provide ideas for further exploration.

The Development of Self-Esteem

There is a consistent developmental progression in the way children conceptualize the self. Young children tend to describe themselves in terms of their physical characteristics ("I wear glasses, I have freckles," and so on) and objective or concrete information ("I am three years old. I live in a house."). As children get older, they consistently mention aspects of their personality in describing themselves ("I am brave, nice, funny," and so on) and their relationships in social groups ("I am in kindergarten. I am a Girl Scout.") (Cobb, 2001; Steinberg & Meyer, 1995).

Children's self-perceptions can directly impact their future. Children with positive self-esteem and self-concept are confident in their ability to meet everyday challenges and are more likely to participate actively in activities. They tend to be independent and free from anxiety, nervousness, excessive worry, tiredness, and loneliness. Children with high self-esteem are also more likely to accept and value others (Steinberg & Meyer, 1995; Stenner & Katzenmeyer, 1976).

★ SELF-CONCEPT/SELF-IMAGE ★

Self-concept or self-image is our perception of who we think we are. It includes the way we think about ourselves in areas such as physical appearance, talents and abilities, popularity and accomplishments (Derman-Sparks, 1991; Klein, 2000; Steinberg & Meyer, 1995). For example, you might see yourself as an early childhood teacher, a piano player, or a person with brown hair.

★ SELF-ESTEEM ★

Self-esteem, on the other hand, refers to the way we feel about ourselves internally and our perceptions of our inner qualities, including self-worth (how valuable we think we are), our life's meaning and purpose, and how appreciated and loved we think we are (Klein, 2000; Steinberg & Meyer, 1995). Feelings of self-esteem also include how we evaluate the traits we associate with ourselves. A person's self-esteem involves an interactive relationship between oneself and the environment. What we believe about ourselves determines how we relate to others; their feedback affects how we feel about ourselves, and how we feel about ourselves affects their feedback (Siccone & Lopez, 2000).

Photography and Self-Esteem

Research has shown that a child's self-image directly influences the development of his or her self-esteem. In other words, to develop high self-esteem, one must begin with a positive view of oneself and a comfort with how one sees oneself (Siccone & Lopez, 2000). A child's

self-esteem begins with self-awareness. By 24 months of age, the majority of children will recognize themselves in a mirror or photograph (Cobb, 2001). At this stage of development, children can clearly distinguish themselves from others and they are increasing their knowledge about themselves, beginning with an awareness of their physical self. As children continue to mature, a concept of self that extends over time will begin to develop. With this awareness, children begin to understand how the self they are seeing now is related to past experiences (Cobb, 2001). Photographs can play an important role in developing this understanding. Reviewing photographs and remembering events and people helps children see themselves as a person with a past, present, and future.

As professionals working with young children, we have a responsibility to help children through the important process of developing their concept of self. We cannot give children self-esteem, but there are ways we can nurture the process of developing it. In addition to treating children respectfully, we can also

★ encourage children to build knowledge and awareness of themselves.

★ help children feel important and cared about by others.

Using photographs in the classroom can help children reach both of these goals. Using photos can help nurture a child's developing self-concept, self-image, and self-esteem in many ways (Woods, 2000), including:

★ Helping children recognize themselves and others in photographs and become comfortable with these images. ("That's me and that's Sasha. She's my best friend!")

★ Allowing children to observe and discuss their development and individuality, as well as the development and individuality of others. ("This is when I was little. I was two. I'm bigger now. I'm four.")

★ Encouraging children to look, share, and discover more about themselves and others. This includes celebrating diversity and recognizing the unique qualities that each person possesses. All of this helps a child in establishing his or her identity. ("We are all different, but some things are the same. Jayla and I both have black hair and Ellie has red.")

Sensitivity to Differences

When using photos in the classroom, children will naturally make observations and compare physical similarities and differences. This offers a good opportunity to stress that while physical differences are normal and help make each of us unique, people are more alike than different.

Photographs are a quick and easy way to give children recognition and put them in the spotlight. The activities in this book help children share information about themselves, explore their feelings, build self-esteem, and more. At the same time, the activities encourage children to learn about their classmates, work together, cooperate, and communicate. All of this helps children come to realize that they are an important part of the classroom community.

We hope that the activities in this book will inspire you to make photographs an important part of your teaching. There are endless possibilities—let your imagination soar!

Incorporating Photographs Into the Classroom

One of the first steps in incorporating photographs into your teaching is to make them a natural part of your classroom environment. Photos provide a unique personal touch that helps children and families feel welcome and comfortable in your classroom. They can be used in any area of the classroom and for many purposes. The key is simply to begin to consider photos as an important part of your classroom environment and to display them in as many areas as possible.

Centers

Take photos of children participating in an activity in each center of the classroom and then display these photos in the center areas. For example, show photos of children building structures with blocks in your block center, playing with puppets in your puppet center, and so on. You might also show photos of students participating in other activities that relate to the center. For example, in your classroom library you might include photos of children visiting the local library.

Bulletin Boards

Incorporate children's photographs into your bulletin boards to showcase children's learning. This helps communicate to families and other visitors what the children in your class are learning. It also gives children a sense of accomplishment and provides a concrete way to help them remember and discuss past experiences. Here are some ideas:

* Display photos of students participating in all kinds of class experiences: art projects, field trips, class performances, and so on.

* Display photos of children participating in a project alongside their finished work. You might also display photos of individual students alongside their recorded comments about the experience.

* Create a rotating display to spotlight a particular child or family. Include photos taken in class as well as ones donated by families.

* Add photos of family members to a family bulletin board. If you are inviting parents to volunteer in your classroom, display photos of parents involved in various class activities.

Photo Albums

Classroom photo albums provide opportunities for children to engage in conversation, develop self-awareness, and build classroom community. Include photos of children participating in classroom activities and invite families to contribute photos from home.

Here are some suggestions:

* Add an album to your classroom library. Invite children to "read" the album and tell stories about the photos to classmates.

* Create an album for your science area that includes photos of children involved in various science activities. Encourage children to look through the album and discuss what they remember about the activities and what they learned.

* Display an album in your block area that shows children with their constructions in various stages of completion. These images can be used in sequencing activities as well.

Classroom Management

Photos can easily be incorporated into classroom management. Photos can be added wherever student names are printed.

* Add photos to name labels for cubbies, desks, mailboxes, and so on. This allows children to be aware of their own space in the classroom and also aids in early literacy development. Seeing their picture with their name helps children recognize and identify their name and later the letters in their name. This also allows them to recognize the names of their classmates.

* Incorporate photos into your classroom birthday display. For example, if you list birthdays on a chart or calendar, include a photo of each child along with his or her birth date.

* Use photos to display daily attendance. For example, when children arrive at school, have them move their photo from one area of the display to another. The photos that have not been moved show at a glance who is absent.

* Have students place their photo on a sign in a center to show that they are working in that area. You might indicate with boxes on the sign how many photos can be placed in each center. This lets children know who is working in each center and when the centers are full.

Documenting Special Events

Photographs are a wonderful way to show what took place at a special event in your classroom. They also help children remember the details of the event. Encourage children to recall events and experiences by helping you retell the sequence of events. This can be done as a large- or small-group activity with a teacher or parent leading the discussion. Invite children each to share something about their photo and their memories of the event, such as their favorite part of the experience.

Photograph family events such as potluck dinners or sing-alongs and display the photos in a place where families will see them when picking up or dropping off their children. This encourages parents and children to discuss the events together and shows families that they are an important part of the classroom community.

If your students participate in classroom or school-wide events to commemorate holidays, take advantage of this photo opportunity. Use the photos to help children recall the

celebration and discuss what they learned about it. This is also an effective way to help children learn about different cultures and to encourage them to share their own cultures with others.

Highlighting Learning Experiences

Take photographs of learning experiences to document your units of study. Then use the photos to help students recall what they have learned and to share learning experiences with their families. Display the photos on bulletin boards or in photo albums (see page 7). You might also incorporate photos into learning experiences in various ways. For example, as part of a study of transportation, have children create a large paper bus and then add their photos to the windows.

Sharing Learning With Parents

As mentioned previously, photographs can be a wonderful way to help parents feel that they are a part of the learning that takes place in your classroom. If parents come into the classroom to pick up or drop off their children, you might create ongoing displays in the classroom or hallway. If parents do not regularly come into the classroom, you might invite them on a regular basis to stop in and see the displays— for example, every Friday afternoon or the first Monday of the month. Or plan special events at which children present their experiences, using the displayed photos as a springboard. These events can be planned presentations or more informal open houses. Either way,

the experience allows children to share an important part of their lives with their families and, in the process, helps them build positive feelings about themselves and their accomplishments.

Photography Tips

Types of Cameras

There are many types of cameras available, any of which will work for the purposes of this book. Disposable cameras, 35mm cameras, Polaroid cameras, and digital cameras are all possibilities. Digital cameras offer the advantages of allowing you to see the photo as you are taking it and erasing unwanted images. Polaroid cameras allow you to develop photos immediately. Choose the type of camera that best fits your needs.

Simple Photography Tips

* To maintain uniformity in photograph size, particularly for close-up face shots, mark a spot on the floor to indicate where each child should stand. Stand in the same place as you are taking the photos.

* Be aware of what is happening in the background when you are taking photos. Consider whether or not the background may distract from your photo, and make adjustments as needed.

* When choosing how to frame a child's image, keep in mind that horizontal shots often work well for face shots and vertical shots work well for body or action shots.

* To vary your images and make them more visually interesting, try changing your perspective as you take pictures. For example, take pictures from above or below the child or from different angles.

* Flashes may reflect in glass or mirrors, affecting the quality of the photo. Use flashes outside when children are in shadows to clarify your images.

* **Safety Note:** Follow the instructions from the camera manufacturer, including the distance you should allow between the flash and the subject.

Let Children Help You

Children love to take photographs and most children older than three years are ready to learn to how to use a camera. Allowing children to share in the photo-taking process and then displaying their photos is a great way to help children feel a sense of accomplishment. Disposable cameras often work best for children's use. As children become more comfortable handling and using a camera, you might consider allowing them to use an inexpensive nondisposable camera.

Cost-Saving Tips

* Order several sets of prints when developing film. This is usually less expensive than having new prints made from negatives and allows you to use the same pictures for several different purposes. Extra prints are also often less expensive than making color copies.

* Ask families to donate film, old cameras, or funds to cover costs of developing film. Families can also help by bringing in coupons for film and photo development.

* Ask families to bring in photos from home to display or use in these activities. These can be family photos or individual photos of children. Be sure to let families know in advance whether or not the photographs will be returned. You might also share the photographs taken at school with families.

* Laminate photos and color copies so that you can use them in several different activities. For example, photos that have been displayed in the classroom can be reused in an activity.

Relax and Enjoy

When you begin using photographs in your classroom, find your comfort level and start simply. Once you see the positive response from your students and families, you can build from there!

Shapes, Numbers, and Letters

Large or Small Group

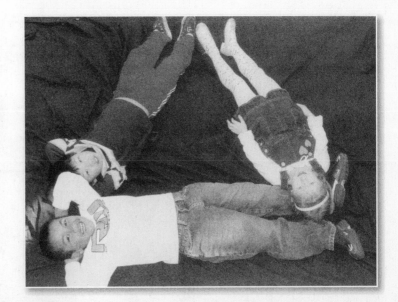

Developmental Focus

★ Cognitive Development: developing spatial awareness; building recognition of shapes; counting; problem solving

★ Social/Emotional Development: cooperating; communicating

Preparation

Determine which shapes, numbers, or letters you will focus on during the activity. (This activity can be done several times in order to focus on one topic at a time.)

Play

1. To introduce the activity, review with children the shapes, numbers, or letters you would like to focus on. You might read aloud a book. (See materials list.)

2. Explain to children that they will work together to create shapes, numbers, or letters with their bodies. Ask children if it would be possible to accomplish this alone or if more than one person is needed.

3. Have children problem-solve with you to figure out how to create each shape, number, or letter with their bodies. This might include counting the number of sides on a shape or the number of lines in a letter or number, determining the

★ MATERIALS ★

- camera
- construction paper
- scissors or paper cutter
- glue stick
- lamination materials or clear contact paper (optional)
- a book about shapes, numbers, or letters (optional), such as:

  The Shape of Things by Dayle Ann Dodds (Candlewick Press, 1994)

  Shapes, Shapes, Shapes by Tana Hoban (Greenwillow, 1986)

  What Comes in 2's, 3's, & 4's? by Suzanne Aker (Simon & Schuster, 1990)

  Chicka Chicka Boom Boom by Bill Martin, Jr. and John Archambault (Simon & Schuster, 1989)

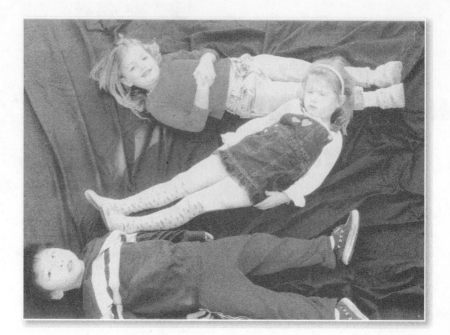

number of children needed, and figuring out how children will need to be positioned. Also discuss the importance of working together, listening, and using words to complete this task.

4. Once children have created each shape, number, or letter, take a photograph of it. You might want to stand at a higher level than the children, using a step stool.

5. Once the photos have printed, mount them on construction paper and laminate them for greater durability.

6. Use the photos to create a bulletin board display or use them for other purposes. (See Variations and Extensions.)

Variations and Extensions

★ Have children work together as a large group to create shapes in various sizes, such as small, medium, and large. If space allows, have the whole class create a large shape together.

★ Create a book of shapes, numbers, or letters using the photos. Add the books to your classroom library.

★ Make two copies of each shape, number, or letter photo, mount them on construction paper, and laminate. Have children use the photo pairs to play a memory game, such as concentration.

★ After forming letters, ask children in each group to brainstorm words that begin with the letter they created.

★ Use the letter or number photos to create an alphabet frieze or number frieze. Display it at eye level in your classroom.

★ Make several copies of the letter photos and create alphabet cards. Have children use the letters to spell their names and other simple words.

★ Use the photos to create number cards. If desired, add number words and dots. Place these cards in the math area with counters such as bears, and have children count the number shown on each card.

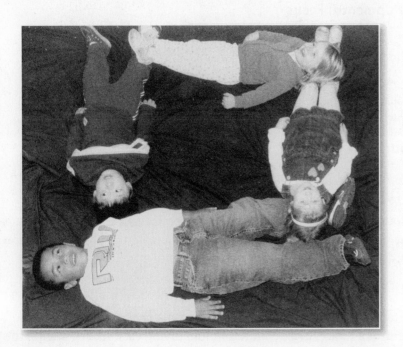

An Alphabet of Friends

Small Group

Developmental Focus

★ Cognitive Development: building recognition of letters; building awareness of the letters in one's name

★ Social/Emotional Development: developing awareness of self and others; building a sense of community; understanding that names represent people

Preparation

1. Create *A* to *Z* letter cards with a large capital and lowercase letter on each card.

2. Mount the photos on construction paper, leaving enough space at the bottom to write children's names. Laminate the photos and letter cards for greater durability.

Play

1. Arrange the letter cards alphabetically on a flat surface, such as the floor or a table. Assist children in identifying each letter (singing the alphabet song is a fun way to do this).

2. Help children find the first letters in their name and in the names of other children. Encourage children to use their photo nameplates.

3. Invite children to match their photo nameplate with the card showing their first initial. To reinforce the connection, have children say "*M* for Matthew" and so on. Then have children match their classmate's nameplates.

Variations and Extensions

★ For more of a challenge, encourage children to name and identify the first letter of their name without referring to their photo nameplate.

★ Once children have mastered identifying and matching first letters of names, encourage them to match the other letters in their name.

★ To promote awareness of others, encourage children to find other students' names that begin with the same letter as their own. Together, count the number of student names that begin with each letter.

★ MATERIALS ★

• small photos, or color copies of photos, of each child (face or body shots)

• construction paper

• scissors or paper cutter

• markers

• glue stick

• lamination materials or clear contact paper (optional)

How Many Friends?

Large or Small Group

Developmental Focus

★ Cognitive Development: building recognition of numbers; counting by rote; counting with one-to-one correspondence

★ Social/Emotional Development: developing awareness of self and others; building a sense of community

Preparation

1. Create large number cards for the numbers you would like to focus on. On one of the cards, include the total number of people in your class (including teachers). Include the corresponding number of dots.

2. Mount the photos on construction paper. For greater durability, laminate the number cards and photos.

Play

1. Help children identify the numbers on the cards, counting the dots for additional reinforcement.

2. Have children count a number of photos to match the number on each card.

3. Together, count all the photos and arrange them together. Discuss the idea of community and explain that all the people in the photos represent your classroom community.

Variations and Extensions

★ To increase self-awareness, include multiple copies of each child's photo so they can count themselves several times.

★ Include photos of other members of your school community (director or principal, teachers, custodians, and so on).

★ Include photos of family members to help children build awareness of the number of members in their family.

★ Introduce the concepts of addition or subtraction by placing two number cards together and asking the child to add or subtract. Encourage them to use the photos as manipulatives to help determine the sum or difference.

MATERIALS

- small photos, or color copies of photos, of each child and teacher (face or body shots)
- construction paper
- scissors or paper cutter
- markers
- dot stickers (optional)
- glue stick
- lamination materials or clear contact paper (optional)

I'm the Opposite!

Large or Small Group

Developmental Focus

★ Cognitive Development: observing; learning about opposites

★ Social/Emotional Development: developing awareness of self and others; cooperating; communicating

Preparation

No preparation is needed.

Play

1. Introduce the concept of opposites. You might want to read a book about the topic. (See materials list.)

2. Explain that children will work together to create photos showing opposites. Together, brainstorm ideas for the photos, such as showing children inside or outside, sitting or standing, frowning or smiling, facing front or facing back, with eyes open or closed, and so on.

3. Involve children in creating the photos. This can be done with pairs, in small groups, or as part of a large-group activity.

4. Mount the printed photos on construction paper and laminate for greater durability. Display the photos on a flat surface, such as the floor or a table. Review the concept of opposites again.

5. Encourage children to discuss what the child is doing in each photo and what the opposite might be. Then invite children to look through the other cards and find the opposite match.

Variations and Extensions

★ For younger children, photograph the same child in each pair of opposites so they can match cards with the same person if they are less comfortable with the concept of opposites.

★ In a small group, lay one card from each pair on a table. Give each child the same number of cards. Ask children to look at their cards and find the opposite card on the table.

MATERIALS

- camera
- construction paper
- glue stick
- scissors or paper cutter
- lamination materials or clear contact paper (optional)
- a book on opposites (optional), such as:
  Olivia's Opposites by Ian Falconer (Atheneum, 2002)
  Opposites by Sandra Boynton (Simon & Schuster, 2001)

Name That Color!

Large or Small Group

Developmental Focus

★ Cognitive Development: building recognition of colors; matching; patterning; observing

★ Social/Emotional Development: cooperating; communicating

Preparation

Gather objects and articles of clothing in each color you wish to focus on. Choose clothing articles that can be put on easily over other clothing, such as large T-shirts, scarves, jackets, and so on.

Play

1. Review colors with children. You might read aloud a book. (See materials list.)

2. Explain to children that they will work together to "create" a scene for each color using clothing and objects. Discuss children's ideas about how they might accomplish this. You might have small groups work together to create a scene for each color.

3. Once children are ready, take a picture of each color scene.

4. Once the pictures have printed, mount them on construction paper and laminate for greater durability. Use the photos for a variety of purposes. (See Variations and Extensions.)

Variations and Extensions

★ As a large-group activity, create a scene with all the colors of the rainbow and take a picture.

★ Post the color photos along with color names around the classroom.

★ Make two copies of each photo, mount them on construction paper, and laminate. Have children use the photo pairs to play a memory game such as concentration.

★ Create cards with color names to use with the pictures in a matching activity.

MATERIALS

- camera
- articles of clothing and objects in different colors
- construction paper
- glue stick
- scissors or paper cutter
- lamination materials or clear contact paper (optional)
- a book about colors (optional), such as:
  Who Said Red? by Mary Serfozo (Margaret K. McElderry Books, 1988)

  Mary Wore Her Red Dress and Henry Wore His Green Sneakers by Merle Peak (Clarion, 1985)

Photo Memory

Small Group

MATERIALS

- double prints of photos, or double color copies of photos, of each child (face or body shots)
- construction paper
- scissors or paper cutter
- glue stick
- lamination materials or clear contact paper (optional)

Developmental Focus

★ Cognitive Development: observing; developing memory skills and spatial awareness; matching; counting

★ Social/Emotional Development: developing awareness of self and others; cooperating; communicating

Preparation

1. Cut the construction paper into cards of the same size.

2. Trim the photos to a uniform size and mount them on the cards. The cards should look identical in size and color when placed facedown.

3. Laminate the cards for greater durability.

Play

1. Arrange the cards facedown on a flat surface, such as a table or the floor.

2. Have children take turns turning over two cards at a time, trying to find two matching photos.

3. If a child makes a match, the child takes another turn. If not, the child returns the cards facedown to their original positions and another child takes a turn.

4. When all the matches have been found, children count their card pairs and name the classmates shown on their cards.

Variations and Extensions

★ Change the object of the game to finding one's own photos rather than finding as many matches as possible.

★ Once a match has been made, invite any of the players to share something special about the child in the photo.

★ Hide one card from each pair somewhere in the classroom. Have children each find a card (either of themselves or another child), return to the group, and take turns finding the matching card.

What's the Pattern?

. . . .

Large or Small Group

CREATE A PATTERN

?

Developmental Focus

★ Cognitive Development: observing; patterning

★ Antibias Awareness: developing awareness of similarities and differences and appreciation for diversity

Preparation

1. Decide which types of patterns you would like children to create, and choose the photos accordingly. For younger children, you might want to focus on basic concepts such as gender and clothing color. For older children, include photos that show similarities in their poses, objects held, settings, activities, expressions, and so on.

2. Mount photos on construction paper and laminate for greater durability.

Play

1. Introduce the concept of patterns. You might demonstrate how to create several simple patterns using blocks, manipulatives, or other objects. Give children the opportunity to determine what would come next in each pattern.

2. Place the photos faceup on a flat surface, such as the floor or a table.

3. Encourage children to look at the photos and notice the similarities and differences in clothing color, poses, and so on.

4. Demonstrate how to create a pattern with the photos, such as boy, girl, boy, girl. Ask children what would come next in the sequence.

5. Once children are comfortable with the concept, invite them to use the photos to create their own patterns.

Variations and Extensions

★ Include photos of family members or pets to use in this activity.

★ For an additional challenge, include objects other than photos. For example, you might create the pattern: photo of a boy, red block, photo of a girl, blue block, photo of a boy, red block, and so on.

MATERIALS

• photos, or color copies of photos, of children (face or body shots; include photos that show similarities, such as color of clothing, items being held, activities, and so on)

• construction paper

• glue stick

• lamination materials or clear contact paper (optional)

• blocks, manipulatives, or other small objects for patterning (optional)

Sensitivity to Differences

Help children understand that while physical differences are normal and help make each of us unique, people are more alike than different.

19

Hidden Friends

Small Group

Developmental Focus

★ Cognitive Development: developing sensory awareness; identifying textures; using vocabulary to describe textures

★ Social/Emotional Development: developing awareness of self and others; cooperating

Preparation

1. Mount the photos on construction paper and laminate.

2. Fill the tubs to a low level with sensory materials.

3. Hide a few photos in each tub of sensory materials.

Play

1. Have children take turns using their hands to dig through the sensory materials, trying to find photos of themselves and their classmates.

2. As children are exploring the materials, encourage them to discuss how the materials feel. Introduce sensory vocabulary such as *hard*, *soft*, *slippery*, *smooth*, *rough*, *light*, and so on.

3. Once children have finished, have them identify whose photos they found. Then have them hide the photos for the next child to take a turn.

Variations and Extensions

★ For a more scientific focus, provide a variety of materials. Encourage children to compare and contrast the sensory experiences and discuss the similarities and differences in how the materials feel.

★ For a mathematics focus, hide multiple photos of children in each tub and ask children to count how many of each friend they found. Then discuss which tub had the most or fewest children, and which child had the most photos in all the tubs.

★ Attach a small magnet or large paper clip to each photo. Provide magnetic wands for children to use as they search through light sensory materials.

MATERIALS

• small photos, or color copies of photos, of each child (face or body shots; multiple copies of each photo may be used)

• construction paper

• glue stick

• scissors or paper cutter

• lamination materials or clear contact paper

• sensory materials, such as sand, shredded paper, and packing foam

• large or small tubs or trays

Plant a Friendship Garden

Large or Small Group

Developmental Focus

★ Cognitive Development: learning about seeds and plants; learning how to care for plants and what they need to grow

★ Social/Emotional Development: developing responsibility; caring for plants; cooperating

Preparation

1. Mount each photo on construction paper or oaktag.

2. Cut out the children in the photos.

3. Laminate each photo and glue it to the top of a craft stick.

Play

1. Discuss seeds and plants and read aloud a book about the topic if desired. (See materials list.) Explain how to plant seeds and care for them. Tell children that they will be planting a class garden.

2. Have children help you prepare the soil for planting.

3. Invite each child to add a seed or seedling plant to your class garden. Once children have planted their seed or plant, invite them to mark their plant with the photo mounted on the stick.

4. Encourage children to continue to care for their plant over time by watering, weeding, and so on.

Variations and Extensions

★ Help children monitor and record the growth of their plants over time. This is a good opportunity to discuss concepts of growth and size and build skills in measuring, comparing, graphing, and so on.

★ To create a family gift, have children plant their seeds or seedlings in empty, clean, individual-sized milk cartons with the tops cut off. Invite children to decorate their "pots" by covering them in construction paper and adding designs with markers or crayons. Have children insert their photo markers in their pots.

MATERIALS

- small photos, or color copies of photos, of each child (face or body shots)

- heavy construction paper or oaktag

- scissors

- glue stick

- lamination materials or clear contact paper

- craft sticks

- large tub for indoor planting (or an outdoor planting space)

- soil

- seeds or seedling plants for each child

- book about plants and seeds (optional), such as: *From Seed to Plant* by Gail Gibbons (Holiday House, 1991)

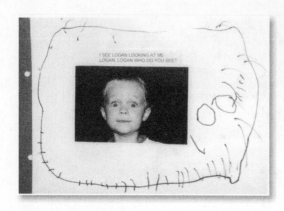

Bookmaking

Large or Small Group

Developmental Focus

★ Cognitive/Linguistic Development: exploring concepts of print and story elements; dictating stories

★ Social/Emotional Development: cooperating; communicating; building a sense of community; developing awareness of self and others

★ Creative Development: creating illustrations; putting together a book

Preparation

1. Determine what kind of book children will create. To introduce the activity, lead a class discussion about the book's topic or read aloud a book on the same topic or with the same format.

2. Cut out the photos of children.

Play

Class Experience

Explain to children that they will be creating a class book about something the class has experienced together, such as a field trip or a special activity. (The photos for this project could be ones taken during the activity or ones of children that can be cut out and added to the book's illustrations.) Lead a discussion about the topic of the book, encouraging children to suggest what information the book could provide. Invite children to create their own page that will include a photo of themselves. Have children dictate the text for their page and add illustrations to their page if desired. Brainstorm a title together and create a cover page. Laminate the pages and bind them together using yarn or staples.

You're the Main Character

Lead a discussion about story characters, defining the concept of main character and providing examples from familiar stories. Then read aloud a story and discuss the main character. Explain to children that they will write their own story in which they are the main character. Have children dictate their stories to you and then add their photos and illustrations to the pages and cover. Laminate the pages and bind them together using yarn or staples.

Re-create Favorite Stories

After reading a favorite story to the class, invite children to re-create the story by adding themselves and their friends to it. Encourage children to change the story as they wish. You might have children work on this individually or in small groups. Have children dictate their stories to you and then add their photos and illustrations to the pages. Display the finished books alongside the original story. Some suggestions of favorite stories to re-create include:

Brown Bear, Brown Bear, What Do You See? by Bill Martin, Jr.
(Holt, Rinehart and Winston, 1967)

Silly Sally by Audrey Wood (Harcourt Brace Jovanovich, 1992)

Chicka Chicka Boom Boom by Bill Martin, Jr. and John Archambault
(Simon & Schuster, 1989)

Variations and Extensions

★ Add the completed books to your classroom library or allow children to take them home to share with family members.

★ Have children act out the completed books for the class or for visitors to your classroom.

★ Provide a variety of photos and other bookmaking materials in a center so that children can continue to create their own books.

Trying Out Different Emotions

Small or Large Group

Developmental Focus

★ Social/Emotional Development: developing awareness of self and others; understanding emotions in oneself and others (exploring what causes different emotions and how people express emotions in different ways, understanding that it is okay to feel and express a variety of emotions, developing comfort in expressing emotions)

★ Antibias Awareness: understanding that people have different emotions; developing awareness that people express emotions in different ways; developing awareness of what may cause people to feel certain emotions and how that may relate to areas of bias

Preparation

No preparation is needed.

Play

1. Lead a discussion about different emotions. Discuss what might make us feel a certain way and how we express our emotions. Ask children to show expressions that portray different emotions. If desired, provide mirrors so that children can see the expressions they are making. You might also read aloud a book that explores this topic. (See materials list.)

2. Explain that each child will have a chance to choose three emotions (or a different number) to express in photos.

3. As you are taking the photos, ask children what feeling they are portraying and what might bring about that feeling.

4. Once the photos have printed, mount them on uniform-sized pieces of construction paper and laminate them for greater durability. Then use them as the basis for further discussion. Have children take turns showing their photos to the group and telling what emotion they were portraying (or ask other students to guess). After looking at each photo, discuss what might make someone feel that way.

Variations and Extensions

★ Use the photos as the basis for a dramatic play activity. Ask children to act out the emotion portrayed in the photo. Or have children use puppets to act out a scene showing what might cause a particular emotion and how puppets might express their feelings.

How Are You Feeling?

Large or Small Group

Developmental Focus

★ Cognitive Development: observing, matching

★ Social/Emotional Development: developing awareness of self and others; understanding emotions in oneself and others (exploring what causes different emotions and how people express emotions, understanding that it is okay to feel and express a variety of emotions, developing comfort in expressing emotions)

★ Antibias Awareness: understanding that people have different emotions; developing awareness that people express emotions in different ways; developing awareness of what may cause people to feel certain emotions and how that may relate to areas of bias

Preparation

1. Create photo cards by mounting the photos on construction paper and laminating them for greater durability. The photo cards can be trimmed to a uniform size or they can vary.

2. Cut four-inch circles from construction paper. On each circle, draw facial features showing an emotion and label the emotion below the face. Some suggestions include happy, sad, angry, afraid, and excited.

Play

1. Lay the photo cards and paper faces faceup on a flat surface, such as the floor or a table, so that all cards are showing.

2. Encourage children to look closely at each photo and describe how the child in the photo might be feeling.

3. Ask children to look for a paper face that shows a similar emotion. Read the label aloud and ask children if this matches. Instead of using paper faces, you might ask children to find another photo that shows a child who might be feeling a similar emotion.

4. Once a match has been made, ask children to discuss what might make someone feel the emotion shown in the two photos.

Variations and Extensions

★ Place some of the photos in a bag and lay the rest on a table. Ask children to take turns drawing a photo from the bag and finding a match with the photos on the table.

★ As children become more comfortable recognizing and discussing emotions, make the activity more challenging by including photos or other pictures of situations that might lead someone to feel a certain way. Have children take turns matching a photo of a situation with a photo showing the emotion it might cause. Encourage children to discuss the relationship between the two photos and explain why the situation might make someone feel a certain way.

★ Have children look in child-safe mirrors as they make expressions showing the different emotions discussed. Ask children to talk about what might make them feel this way.

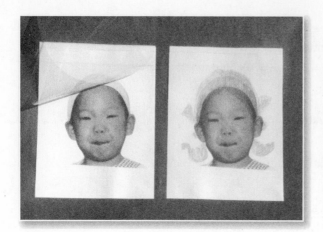

Changing Yourself

Small Group

★ MATERIALS ★

- enlarged color copies of photos of each child (face shots, approximately $8\frac{1}{2}$ by 11 inches)

- clear overhead transparencies

- tape

- washable, nontoxic dry-erase markers

- paper towels or soft cloths

- child-safe mirrors (optional)

Developmental Focus

★ Social/Emotional Development: developing self-awareness; becoming comfortable seeing oneself as one usually appears as well as in new and different ways

★ Antibias Awareness: experiencing what it might be like to look different than one usually does; developing awareness of others

★ Creative Development: using a variety of materials for self-expression

Preparation

Mount each photo on construction paper. Attach an overlay to each photo.

Play

1. Demonstrate how to use dry-erase markers to change a photo by drawing additional features and details on the overlay. For example, add a moustache, change the hair color, add glasses, change the shape of the eyebrows, and so on. Encourage children to be creative and have fun!

2. Show children how to use the cloths or towels for erasing. Children can wipe off the marker as many times as desired and make new changes.

3. Once children are satisfied with their work, have them compare the photo beneath the overlay with the new image. Ask children to discuss how they see themselves in the photo and with the overlay. If desired, provide mirrors for children to compare how they usually look with their changed image.

Variations and Extensions

★ Once children are comfortable changing themselves, have them work with a partner and change each other. Partners can then discuss how they feel about the changes made in their own picture.

★ Make several color copies of each child (full-page face shots or body shots) and place them in the art area. Encourage children to repeat this activity and try different techniques using images of themselves or their friends.

★ Instead of using overlays, have children use collage materials directly on a large color copy of a face shot mounted on construction paper. Encourage children to change themselves by coloring the photo, drawing details with markers, and gluing on yarn for hair, cut paper or fabric for hats, and so on.

Build a "Photo" Graph

Large or Small Group

Developmental Focus

★ Cognitive Development: collecting and analyzing data; graphing; counting; comparing; one-to-one correspondence

★ Social/Emotional Development: cooperating; communicating; sharing information about oneself

★ Antibias Awareness: developing awareness of similarities and differences; developing appreciation for diversity; learning about other students and their families

Preparation

Cut the photos to a size that will fit in the squares on your graph.

Play

1. Choose a topic for your chart or graph, such as "How We Get to School," "Favorite Animals," and so on. You might choose a topic based on a current topic of study or a topic you would like to introduce. Or you might ask children for suggestions and then have them vote for the topic they would like.

2. Write the title at the top of the chart paper. As a group, brainstorm possible responses. Then write these in the left-hand column. You might add picture icons to each response. Help children determine where on the chart to place their photo, based on their response. Encourage children to express their response to the group before attaching their photo to the appropriate space on the graph.

3. Review and discuss the completed graph as a group. You might count and compare each of the responses, note similarities and differences, and discuss the value of diversity. Leave the graph on display for further discussion and observation.

Variations and Extensions

★ Involve families in this activity by inviting them to contribute to the data graphed or by adding family pictures to the graph.

Self-Portraits

Small Group

Developmental Focus

★ Cognitive Development: observing; building spatial awareness

★ Social/Emotional Development: developing awareness of self and others; becoming comfortable with one's appearance

★ Antibias Awareness: developing awareness of similarities and differences; developing appreciation for diversity

★ Creative Development: building comfort and confidence using artistic materials; using self-expression and creativity

Preparation

Set out the art supplies for children's use.

Play

1. Invite children to explore the photos of themselves and then create a self-portrait using any combination of materials. You might also have children observe themselves in mirrors.

2. Discuss facial features and encourage children to observe where their facial features are located in relation to each other and to the shape of their face (eyes above the nose, mouth below the nose, and so on). Also encourage children to note their eye, hair, and skin color. Invite children to represent themselves creatively in any way they choose.

3. Display the completed self-portraits along with children's photos. Lead a discussion noting children's unique artistic expressions and celebrating diversity. You might also read aloud a book. (See materials list.)

Variations and Extensions

★ Pair children and encourage them to observe their partner and their partner's photograph. Then invite children to create a portrait of their partners.

MATERIALS

- photos, or color copies of photos, of each child (face or body shots; enlarged photos work well)

- art supplies, such as paper, washable tempera paint, watercolors, markers, crayons, scissors, glue, and so on

- child-safe mirrors (optional)

- a book about diversity, such as:
  All the Colors of the Earth by Sheila Hamanaka (HarperTrophy, 1999)
  The Colors of Us by Karen Katz (Henry Holt, 1999)

Sensitivity to Differences

Help children understand that while physical differences are normal and help make each of us unique, people are more alike than different.

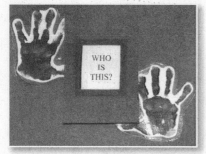

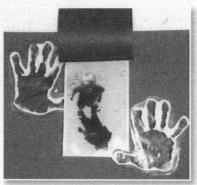

My Hands and Feet

Large or Small Group

MATERIALS

- photo, or color copy of photo, of each child (face or body shot, any size)
- pencils and markers or finger paint
- scissors
- construction paper
- tape

Sensitivity to Differences

Help children understand that while physical differences are normal and help make each of us unique, people are more alike than different.

Developmental Focus

★ Cognitive Development: observing; counting; measuring

★ Social/Emotional Development: developing awareness of self and others; developing comfort with one's physical appearance

★ Antibias Awareness: developing awareness of similarities and differences; developing appreciation for diversity

Preparation

No preparation is needed.

Play

1. Have children trace their hands or feet (or both). As an alternative, have children make hand- or footprints using finger paint. Allow the paint to dry. Cut out the prints and mount them on construction paper in a contrasting color.

2. Attach photographs of children beside their handprints or footprints. If desired, attach a flap over the photo so that children can play a guessing game.

3. To reinforce math concepts, have children measure their hands and feet and count fingers and toes.

Variations and Extensions

★ Invite each child to show their handprint and footprint to the group and share something they like to do using their hands and feet.

★ Cut out the handprints or footprints and help children use them to measure short distances.

 **Is Me!**

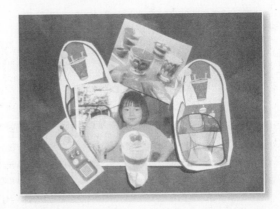

Small Group

Developmental Focus

★ Social/Emotional Development: developing awareness of oneself and others; sharing information about oneself; learning about others

★ Antibias Awareness: developing awareness of similarities and differences; developing appreciation for diversity

★ Creative Development: using self-expression and creativity; building comfort and confidence using artistic materials

Preparation

Attach each child's photo to the center of a sheet of construction paper. (Older children may want to do this themselves.)

Play

1. Invite children to make a collage about themselves. Encourage them to think about things they like, such as foods, activities, animals, colors, and so on. Have children draw or cut pictures from magazines showing things they like. Once they have collected a variety of pictures, show children how to glue the pictures around their photo to create a collage.

2. As children are working, initiate conversations with them about their interests, using their pictures as a starting point.

3. Display the completed collages in the classroom. Discuss similarities and differences among the collages. You might point out how it is nice that some children like some of the same things and some like different things. You might also want to comment how everyone has made their collage in their own way and that no two collages look the same. This is a great activity to build classroom community at the beginning of the year. Children enjoy seeing collages made by their teachers as well.

Variations and Extensions

★ Invite each child to share their completed collage with the whole group and tell about themselves. Invite children to ask each other questions.

★ Have pairs of children work together to create a shared collage about both of them, or they can create a collage about their partners.

MATERIALS

• photo, or color copy of photo, of each child (face or body shot, any size)

• 11- by 17-inch construction paper

• glue

• old magazines or pictures cut from magazines

• child-safe scissors

• markers and crayons

All Twisted Up

Small Group

Developmental Focus

★ Social/Emotional Development: cooperating; communicating; developing awareness of self and others; developing comfort with one's own body

★ Physical Development: developing gross-motor skills, spatial awareness, body awareness, flexibility, coordination, muscle strength, and balance; learning concepts of left and right

Preparation

1. Laminate each large photo. Mount the laminated photos on oaktag or thin cardboard. Attach a photo to each circle on the Twister™ board or to the floor with duct tape.

2. Mount the small photos on construction paper. Place these in a paper bag. Draw a hand or foot on several small squares of construction paper. Write either *L* for left or *R* for right on each square. Place these in a separate paper bag.

3. Clear a large space on the floor.

Play

1. Choose a leader for the game (a child or teacher) and determine a playing order (who goes first, second, and so on).

2. Have the leader choose a photo from one bag and a square from the other. The leader then directs the first player how to move as indicated by the photo and square. For example, if the leader chooses a picture of Maria and a foot with the letter *L*, the leader tells the player, "Place your left foot on Maria." The player steps with the left foot on the photo of Maria.

3. The leader returns the photo and square to their bags and directs the next player in the same way.

4. If a player loses balance, the player steps out and rejoins the game on the next turn. The game continues until each player has had several turns.

Variations and Extensions

★ For younger children, omit the right and left directions. Instead say, for example, "Place one foot on Maria."

MATERIALS

- enlarged photos, or color copies of photos, of each child (face or body shots)

- small photos, or color copies of photos, of each child (face or body shots)

- lamination materials or clear contact paper

- oaktag or thin cardboard

- glue stick

- Twister™ board game (optional)

- duct tape or other strong tape

- construction paper

- scissors

- markers

- 2 paper bags

Balance Yourself or a Friend

Large or Small Group

Developmental Focus

* Social/Emotional Development: developing awareness of self and others; developing comfort with one's own body
* Physical Development: developing body awareness, spatial awareness, coordination, and balance

Preparation

Attach the photos to beanbags using tape or clear contact paper.

Play

1. Discuss the concept of balancing and model how to balance a beanbag on various parts of your body (head, arms, legs, hands, feet, and so on).

2. Show children the beanbags with photos on them. Encourage children to practice balancing themselves or a friend on various parts of their body.

Variations and Extensions

* Have children work in pairs. Give each pair the beanbags with their photos on them. Have each child balance the beanbag with his or her partner's photo on it. Instruct partners to give directions about where to balance the beanbag—for example, balance the beanbag on your head, arm, and so on.

* Play music while the children are balancing. Encourage them to walk or move to the beat of the music while balancing their beanbags.

* Challenge children to try to balance more than one "friend" at a time, either on the same body part (for example, three beanbags on your leg) or on different body parts (for example, one beanbag on your head and one on your foot).

> ### MATERIALS
>
> * small photos, or color copies of photos, of each child (face shots)
> * tape or clear contact paper
> * small beanbags

Hide and Seek

Large or Small Group

Developmental Focus

★ Social/Emotional Development: developing awareness of self and others; cooperating; communicating

★ Physical Development: developing body coordination, body awareness, and spatial awareness

Preparation

Mount the photos on construction paper. Laminate for greater durability.

Play

1. This game can be played inside or outside and is similar to the traditional game of hide and seek, except that photos are hidden. One person (teacher or child) is designated as the "seeker." The seeker closes his or her eyes and counts to a designated number while the other players each hide a photo of themselves somewhere in the game area.

2. Once the seeker has finished counting, the seeker searches the game area for photos. The seeker attempts to find as many friends as possible. The other players give the seeker clues about where their pictures are hidden.

Variations and Extensions

★ Have children play the game with a partner. Give each pair of children photos of themselves. Each partner takes turns being the seeker while the other partner hides the photos of both partners.

★ One person (teacher or child) can act as the "hider" while the rest of the group closes their eyes. Then children look for their own photo or for photos of friends. To make this even more challenging, the hider can give each seeker a clue about whose photo they should find. For example, "Find a friend who wears glasses and has one sister."

★ Play the game with numerous photos, including former classmates, other teachers, family members, and so on. Have children work together to find all the photos. Once all the photos have been found, invite children to share something special about the person (or people) whose photo they found.

Dance With a Partner

Large or Small Group

Developmental Focus

★ Social/Emotional Development: developing comfort and confidence with one's movements and with dancing in front of others

★ Antibias Awareness: developing awareness of similarities and differences in people's movements

★ Physical Development: developing body awareness, spatial awareness, flexibility, coordination, and rhythm

★ Creative Development: expressing oneself freely through movement

Preparation

Mount the photos on construction paper and laminate for greater durability.

Play

1. Give children photos either of themselves or a friend.

2. Play the music and invite children to dance with their photo "partners." Encourage them to move in any way they choose. This is a very open-ended experience encouraging creative expression.

Variations and Extensions

★ Stop the music periodically and invite children to share something special about the child whose photo they are holding. Or invite children to exchange photos each time the music stops.

★ Build specific motor skills by introducing various dance movements for children to try as they dance with their photos.

MATERIALS

• enlarged photos, or color copies of photos, of each child (face or body shots)

• construction paper

• glue stick

• scissors or paper cutter

• lamination materials or clear contact paper (optional)

• a variety of upbeat musical selections, such as children's music, bluegrass, classical, and so on

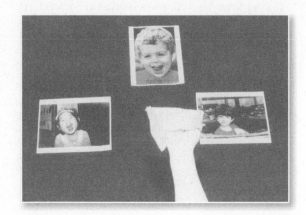

Toss to a Friend

Large or Small Group

Developmental Focus

★ Social/Emotional Development: developing awareness of self and others; cooperating

★ Physical Development: developing spatial awareness and eye-hand coordination

Preparation

Mount each photo on construction paper and laminate for greater durability.

Play

1. Arrange the photos in a line or randomly on the floor or the ground.

2. Invite children to toss their beanbag onto the photo of themselves or a friend. Encourage children to try to aim their beanbag so it lands directly on the photo.

Variations and Extensions

★ For more of a challenge, use smaller photos or place them further away from children.

★ Invite each child to choose a friend's photo to toss to. Encourage the child to share something special about that friend before or after making their toss.

★ Play music while children are playing the game. Encourage them to listen to the music and toss gently to the beat of the music.

★ Place the photos in the squares of a hopscotch board. To take a turn, a player tosses a beanbag on a photo and then hops to the end of the board, hopscotch style. Encourage children to share something special about the friend they landed on.

MATERIALS

• photos, or color copies of photos, of each child (any size, face or body shots)

• construction paper

• glue stick

• scissors or paper cutter

• lamination materials or clear contact paper (optional)

• beanbags or other soft items to toss

Musical Friends

Large or Small Group

Developmental Focus

★ Social/Emotional Development: developing awareness of oneself and others; cooperating

★ Physical Development: developing spatial awareness, body awareness, and coordination

Preparation

1. Mount the photos on construction paper and laminate for greater durability.

2. Tape the photos on chairs or carpet squares. You will need a chair or carpet square for each player. (This version eliminates the safety issues of the traditional version in which there are not enough seats for players.) Arrange the chairs or carpet squares in a circle. If using chairs, arrange them facing out with the backs touching.

Play

1. Play music and invite children to walk around the seats. When the music stops, have children sit on a seat near them. (Remind children not to run and explain that there is a seat for each child.)

2. Give each child an opportunity to identify the classmate they have landed on. You might also invite children to share something special about that classmate (or themselves if they landed on their own photograph).

Variations and Extensions

★ Older children may enjoy playing in the traditional manner where one person sits out each round. Each time the music stops, draw a child's name or photo out of a bag. Whoever landed on that person sits out. Remove one chair or carpet square each round so the number of seats is equal to the number of players still in the game.

★ Play a variety of types of music and discuss the different styles.

★ Use family photos instead of children's photos. Encourage children to identify whose family they have landed on.

MATERIALS

- enlarged photos, or color copies of photos, of each child (face or body shots)
- construction paper
- glue stick
- scissors or paper cutter
- lamination materials or clear contact paper (optional)
- chairs or carpet squares (one per child)
- duct tape
- a variety of upbeat musical selections, such as jazz, pop, bluegrass, classical, and so on

Find Your Face

Small Group

Sensitivity to Differences

Help children understand that while physical differences are normal and help make each of us unique, people are more alike than different.

Developmental Focus

★ Cognitive Development: developing spatial awareness; observing; matching; problem solving

★ Social/Emotional Development: developing awareness of self and others; developing comfort with one's appearance; cooperating; sharing

★ Antibias Awareness: developing awareness of similarities and differences; developing appreciation for diversity

Preparation

1. Mount each photo on construction paper.

2. Cut each photo into several pieces. For a simpler puzzle, create pieces that are uniform in size and shape, such as strips. (You might use a paper cutter for this.) For more of a challenge, create pieces of varied size and shape.

3. Laminate the pieces for greater durability.

Play

1. Arrange all the puzzle pieces faceup on a flat surface, such as a table or the floor.

2. Invite children to find the pieces to make their own face or a friend's face.

Variations and Extensions

★ To make the activity more challenging, include full-body or action shots, or photos that include more than one child.

★ Create a puzzle using an enlarged photo of the whole class. Have children find themselves in a puzzle piece. Invite children to each put a piece of the puzzle in place.

Mixed-up Faces

Large or Small Group

Developmental Focus

★ Cognitive Development: developing spatial awareness; observing; matching; problem solving

★ Social/Emotional Development: developing awareness of self and others; sharing; cooperating

★ Antibias Awareness: developing awareness of similarities and differences; developing appreciation for diversity; developing comfort with one's appearance

Preparation

1. Mount each photo on construction paper.

2. Cut the photos into uniform shapes, such as strips or squares. (Use a paper cutter to cut several puzzles at once.) For a simpler puzzle, cut each photo into two pieces. For a more complicated puzzle, cut more pieces. Make the pieces for each facial feature identical in size and shape. For example, all the mouth pieces should be the same size and shape, and so on. Laminate for greater durability.

Play

1. Spread out the puzzle pieces faceup on a flat surface, such as the floor or a table. Either arrange them randomly or group pieces by facial feature, such as all the eyes together, noses together, and so on.

2. Encourage children to create new and interesting faces by combining parts of different faces. For example, to create new face, a child might choose a nose from one photo, a mouth from a second photo, and eyes from a third.

Variations and Extensions

★ Working together in a large group, have each child take a turn adding a feature to each new face that is created. Lead a discussion about working together and contributing to the finished product.

★ For variety, place the puzzle pieces in a large bag or box. Have students draw pieces one by one and add these to the faces they are creating.

MATERIALS

- enlarged photos, or color copies of photos, of each child (same size face shots)
- construction paper
- glue stick
- scissors or paper cutter
- lamination materials or clear contact paper (optional)

Sensitivity to Differences

Help children understand that while physical differences are normal and help make each of us unique, people are more alike than different.

Create-a-Face Notebook

Small Group

MATERIALS

- 8½- by 11-inch color copies of photos of each child (face shots)
- construction paper
- glue stick
- hole punch or three-hole punch
- scissors or paper cutter
- lamination materials or clear contact paper (optional)
- three-ring notebook

Sensitivity to Differences

Help children understand that while physical differences are normal and help make each of us unique, people are more alike than different.

Developmental Focus

★ Cognitive Development: developing spatial awareness; observing; matching

★ Social/Emotional Development: developing awareness of self and others; developing comfort with one's appearance

★ Antibias Awareness: developing awareness of similarities and differences; developing appreciation for diversity

Preparation

1. Mount each photo on construction paper.

2. Punch three holes along the left side of the photo so that it will fit in a three-ring notebook. (Using a three-hole punch works best.)

3. Cut each photo into three symmetrical strips, using a paper cutter for uniformity. There should be a hole on each piece.

4. Laminate the pieces for greater durability. Punch the holes through the plastic.

5. Insert the pieces in the three-ring notebook to create each face.

Play

1. Encourage children to look through the notebook of faces. Ask them to find themselves and notice the different parts of their face.

2. Invite children to mix and match the pieces to create new faces.

Variations and Extensions

★ To add variety, add photos of teachers or parents as well. Photos with beards or mustaches are especially fun!

★ If you have had students leave your class, add their photos to the notebook as a way to help students remember them.

A Plethora of Puppets

Large or Small Group

Developmental Focus

★ Social/Emotional Development: developing awareness of self and others; role playing; cooperating; communicating

★ Physical Development: developing fine-motor skills

★ Creative Development: using self-expression and creativity; presenting yourself in new ways

Preparation

Follow the assembly instructions below for each type of puppet.

Stick Puppets: Mount each face or full-body photo on construction paper, cut out the photos of children, and laminate. Tape or glue a craft stick to the back of the puppet.

Paper Plate Puppets: Mount enlarged full-face photos on paper plates. Tape or glue a craft stick to the back of the puppet.

Sock Puppets: Mount enlarged photos of faces on construction paper, cut out the faces, and laminate. Attach each face to a sock using strong tape or a glue gun (for adult use only). If desired, decorate the sock with fabric scraps for clothes.

Finger Puppets: Mount small photos of faces on construction paper, cut out the faces, and laminate. Attach the photos to the fingers of a glove using tape or a glue gun (for adult use only). Or attach the photo to a paper ring.

Paper Dolls: Mount enlarged full-body photos on construction paper, cut out the figures, and laminate. Tape or glue craft sticks to the back. Invite children to create paper clothes to tape on the puppet.

MATERIALS

- face or whole-body photos, or color copies, of each child (face or body shots)
- construction paper
- paper plates
- craft sticks
- tape or glue
- glue gun (optional, for adult use only)
- lamination materials or clear contact paper
- child-safe scissors
- old, clean socks and gloves
- cardboard boxes
- small paper cups
- helium balloons
- string
- vehicle toys
- dollhouses or blocks and other props (See Home, Sweet Home, page 44.)

Play

Use any of the puppets in the following ways.

Set the Stage: Use a premade puppet stage or create a small or large stage using cardboard boxes of various sizes. Encourage children to use their puppets to act out favorite stories or create new stories.

Up, Up, and Away! Have each child decorate a small paper cup to use as a hot-air balloon gondola and then place a small puppet or photo inside. Attach a helium balloon to the rim of the cup and a string to the bottom or side of the cup. Invite children to hold the string and guide their flights. Encourage children to imagine and discuss where they are traveling, how long it will take to reach their destination, what it is like flying in the hot-air balloon, and so on. You might also play music while children are guiding their flights.

Let's Go for a Ride: Tape small puppets inside vehicle toys such as cars or trucks. Adjust the size of the puppet to the size of the vehicle. Encourage children to playact a trip that they are taking either by themselves or with friends.

Home, Sweet Home: To encourage playacting, provide dollhouses for children to use with small puppets. Or provide a variety of blocks and other props so that children can create their own settings. You might include toy furniture, small boxes, small plastic animals, carpet scraps or artificial grass, silk plants or flowers, and so on. Encourage children to create any kind of setting for their puppets.

Variations and Extensions

★ Invite children to use their puppets during large-group time. This is a nice way to give children the opportunity to express themselves in front of the group in a comfortable way.

★ Encourage children to act out their favorite stories using a puppet of themselves to portray the main character.

Put Yourself in a Setting

Small Group

Developmental Focus

★ Social/Emotional Development: developing awareness of self and others; role-playing; cooperating; communicating

★ Physical Development: developing fine-motor skills

★ Creative Development: using self-expression and creativity; presenting oneself in new ways

Preparation

1. Mount the setting photos on construction paper and laminate them for greater durability.

2. Cut out objects and animals from photos or magazines. These might relate to the settings, such as animals that live in a particular habitat, camping gear, a spaceship, safari hats, and so on.

3. Cut out the photos of children.

Play

1. Have children work in small groups or individually. Provide each group with several settings and cut-out objects. Give each group photos of the children in that group.

2. Invite children to choose a setting and playact, using their photos within that setting. Encourage children to use the cut-out objects in the setting as well. Explain to children that they can move on to a different setting when they are ready.

Variations and Extensions

★ Look for photos of settings that relate to a topic of study, such as oceans, deserts, rain forests, cities, outer space, or places in the neighborhood or school.

★ Invite children to dictate a story based on their playacting.

★ Have children draw or paint their own settings.

MATERIALS

- photos, or color copies of photos, of each child (full-body shots)

- enlarged photos of settings or photos cut from magazines (8 by 10 inches or larger)

- photos of various objects and animals or photos cut from magazines (These might relate to the setting photos.)

- construction paper

- tape or glue

- scissors or paper cutter

- lamination materials or clear contact paper (optional)

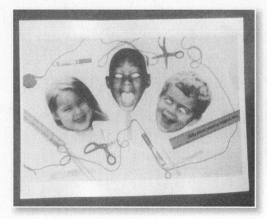

Photo Masks

Small Group

MATERIALS

- enlarged photos, or color copies of photos, of each child (face shots)

- craft supplies to decorate masks, such as markers, glue, tissue paper, yarn, and so on

- paper plates or heavy construction paper

- glue sticks

- scissors

- exacto knife (optional; for adult use only)

- lamination materials or clear contact paper (optional)

- large craft sticks or string

- child-safe mirrors

Developmental Focus

★ Social/Emotional Development: developing awareness of self and others; role-playing; cooperating; communicating

★ Physical Development: developing fine-motor skills

★ Creative Development: using self-expression and creativity; presenting yourself in new ways; building comfort and confidence using artistic materials

Preparation

No preparation is needed.

Play

1. Give children a photo of themselves. Help children turn the photos into masks by mounting them on plates or heavy paper, attaching craft sticks to the backs, and cutting out eye holes. (An adult should cut the eye holes. An exacto knife works well for this purpose.)

2. Invite children to decorate their mask in any way they like using the materials provided.

Variations and Extensions

★ Encourage children to playact as they wear their masks, then exchange masks with friends and teachers. Discuss what it is like pretending to be someone else.

★ Invite children to prepare a performance using their masks.

Photo Blocks

Small Group

Developmental Focus

★ Cognitive Development: developing spatial awareness; observing; problem solving

★ Social/Emotional Development: developing awareness of self and others; sharing; cooperating; communicating

★ Physical Development: developing fine-motor skills and eye-hand coordination

Preparation

1. Cut each photograph to a size that will fit on a block.

2. Attach the photos to the blocks using clear contact paper. Leave some blocks uncovered.

Play

1. Present children with the blocks (both with photos and without).

2. Encourage children to play with the blocks and build with them in any way they choose.

Variations and Extensions

★ Invite children to dictate a narrative about what they built, how they built it, what "friends" were included in their structure, and anything else they would like to share about the process or product.

★ Create photo blocks using photos of children who are no longer in the class or photos of family members.

★ Leave the blocks in the block area. Periodically add new photo blocks to the area.

★ For a large-group activity, invite children to work together to build a structure with the blocks. Have each child add to a class creation. At the end, ask children to share what they or others contributed to the creation.

> ## MATERIALS
>
> • small photos, or color copies of photos, of each child (face or body shots)
>
> • scissors
>
> • blocks of various sizes and types
>
> • clear contact paper

Bibliography

Cobb, Nancy J. *The Child: Infants and Children*. Mountain View, CA: Mayfield Publishing Company, 2001.

Derman-Sparks, Louise. "Self-Esteem: Helping Children Feel Good About Themselves . . . and Others, Too." *Scholastic Pre-K Today*. November/December 1991, 36–42.

Klein, H. A. "Self-Esteem and Beyond." *Childhood Education* 76 no. 4 (2000): 240.

Siccone, Frank, and Lilia Lopez. *Educating The Heart: Lessons to Build Respect and Responsibility*. Needham Heights, Massachusetts: Allyn & Bacon, 2000.

Steinberg, Laurence, and Roberta Meyer. *Childhood*. New York: McGraw-Hill, Inc., 1995.

Stenner, A. J., and W. G. Katzenmeyer. "Self-Concept Development in Young Children." *Phi Delta Kappa* 58 (1976). 356–357.

Woods, Carol S. "A Picture Is Worth a Thousand Words: Using Photographs in the Classroom." *Young Children*. September 2000, 82–84.